I0791472
Approximately one third of the food we eat is the result of honey bee pollination.

In their 6–8 week lifespan, a worker bee will fly the equivalent distance of 1 ½ times the circumference of the Earth.

A single bee will produce only about 1/12 of a teaspoon of honey in its lifetime.

Honey bees are the only insect that produces food consumed by humans.

BEARDED BEE

BUMBLE BEE

During a collection trip, a honey bee will visit anywhere from 50 to 100 flowers.

In ancient Egypt, people paid their taxes with honey.

Honey bees are not born knowing how to make honey. They are taught in the hive by older bees.

Bees can be trained to locate buried land mines.

In order to make a pound of honey, a hive of bees must fly 55,000 miles.

Bee venom is used as a treatment for ailments, including arthritis and high blood pressure.

Honey bees beat their wings 200 times per second, creating the "buzz" sound.

Bees are one of the most studied creatures and written about animals.

On average, an American consumes
1.31 pounds of honey every year.

CUCKOO BEE

A single hive can produce anywhere from 60 to 100 pounds of honey every year.

In Greek mythology, Apollo is the first beekeeper.

The ancient Greeks and Romans viewed honey as a symbol of love, beauty, and fertility.

THANK YOU.
THE END.

COPYRIGHT 2020
BY EDDIE ALFARO
ALL RIGHTS RESERVED.

MORE BOOKS AT:

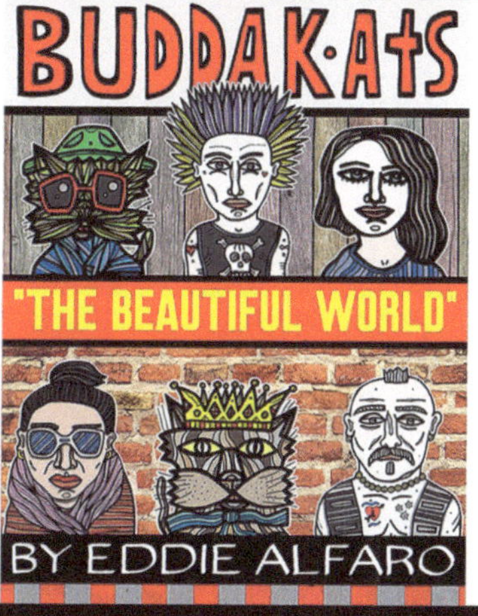

631ART.COM

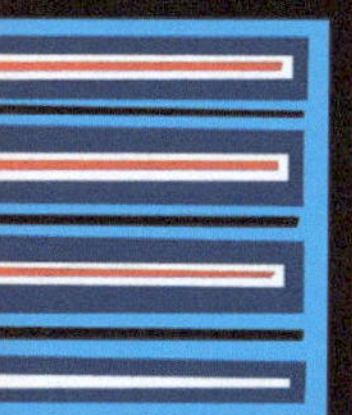

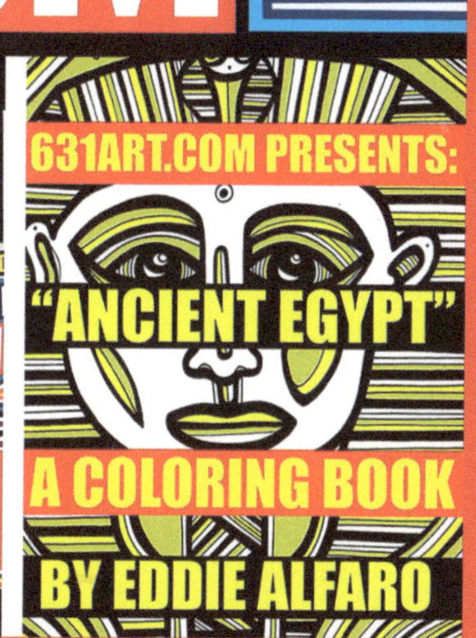